A Woman Milking

Barnyard Poems

Also by Marcia Slatkin

A Season's Milking
I Kidnap My Mother

A Woman Milking

Barnyard Poems

Poems by Marcia Slatkin

Word Press

Published by Word Press
P.O. Box 541106
Cincinnati, OH 45254-1106

Typeset in Goudy by WordTech Communications LLC, Cincinnati, OH

ISBN: 1933456493
LCCN: 2006938853

Poetry Editor: Kevin Walzer
Business Editor: Lori Jareo

Cover art: Eleanor Meier

Visit us on the web at www.word-press.com

The author thanks editors of the following publications in which some of these poems appeared: *Xanadu, Bizzaro/Dobrin/ Slatkin* by Backstreet Editions, *Street Magazine, Zephyr, Brook Spring, Sunrust, Paris Review, Live Poets, Oberon,* the chapbook published by Pudding House Press called *A Season's Milking, The Light of City and Sea* by Street Press, and thanks to Marga Richter, who set six of these poems to music: *Six songs for mezzo soprano and piano*

With love and thanks
to Heidi, Becky and Van
who were part of it,
to the goats, ducks and hens
for their naked honesty,
to Ellie, for art and friendship;
to Cortney, Carin, Adelle, Myriam
for critical strength, and infusions of courage;
and to Dan, my home base.

Contents

Spring

Spring Cleaning

Winter
   is soaped
     with the suds
       of a blustering squall.

Sear leaves
   are crushed
               by sodden flakes,
       black boughs
   are steeped
               in foaming bleach,

               and spinning dryers
       green the world

as light
   flicks dusk
       from naked trees

Labor

It starts: a splash
stains your udder.
I see jutting neon teats.
Your grunts plead.

I stroke your nose
and offer feed
as a man's hand
invades the space
where hooves and head
are late. He tugs

your half-born, wet,
from your womb.
Neck bells
bash your teats
as you turn
to lick its feet.

One last twist
and the stall is a morgue,
your bleat a scream.
Young bones snapped,
your blood and sap
splash to the straw.

    Next day,

your milk is rich.
my fingers ache
with the taking.
I buy ducks as company,
and their twittering distracts you.

But often,
you sniff the straw, lick
the walls, paw the ground
for all that's hidden, lost,
that was yours.

Cloud

He passed through May
like a cloud.

Born too soon,
skin stung by straw
and the grate of a mother's
tongue, his eyelids
fought off morning light.

Hooves translucent,
long legs folded on fur
white as dandelion fleece,

he could not even swallow milk
I dropped behind his tongue.

His lungs pumped
in sporadic gusts.

Hands
forced food
down tubes.
He drowned.
His round eyes glazed.

I felt him spread
and slowly drift away.

The skin I held
turned lumpy, cold—
a matted doll
sparsely stuffed with clay.

Sickness

Twice a day it is the same:
I swab goat skin,
pink beneath the fur,
my arm taut
before the sharp steel sinks.

Everywhere I go, I practice:
car wipers are needles,
the shift stick a quick plunger.
My wrist arcs
as it attacks air.

How I dread it:
a pull into traffic,
a dive deep under,
a leap from a wrong train—

space
between now
and after.

Comfort

Some nights
I come to visit,
both of us middle-aged
and missing our children.

The sour smell of udder
seeps through fog.

At leisure now,
unlike the pump and clatter
of morning milking,
we stroll.

All signposts torn
during our great sorrow,
we will not roam alone.
I hold branches down,
you lick my hand,
and browse.

In the stall,
I add straw,
yet you paw, bleat,
lick walls soaked
with the scent you seek,
search the hay for clues,
plead with any shape you see—

and finally
retreat to sleep.

Adolescence

Before the drake
first chased her,
before a yolk formed
in her wet, swelling space, before
she ever felt the smooth shell
of egg between her legs,

the young duck

(sweet as Lolita
feeling the first
bloom of breasts,
touching them absently,
gazing at mirrors
with parted lips)

stopped
before
the eggs of hens
and watched them,

feeling her feathers
rise and fall, feeling
her heart beat, feeling
a sense of roundness
merge with her future—

the young duck,
motionless,
watched.

Couples

They are always together.

Their down shapes
circle and close
as their beaks peck grain,
Pekings shifting
with the synchronicity
of migrating birds.

As their necks arch to drink,
their matched movements
seem to mime desire,

as ours do,
our thoughts
shifting and delicate
as the space
between their petaled
backs. And when

our bodies
circle and close,
we too slake thirst—
as wet wings arc
toward pleasure.

A Barnyard of Women

I fight with my love,
curse, cry,
find your stall,
sit on tawny straw
and practice my "good-bye."

You look in through the barn door,
ears high, eyes wide,
goat nose sniffing me,
tongue licking my thigh,
your love coarse
as a wash cloth.

Then two hens—

stately
in the saffron light,
burnished claws
aglow,

perch nearby
as we cluck
our freedom
from the crowing bravado
of cocks.

Mid-Wifery

A splash of warm and wet—

and then a slippery,
silent doe: A barely
beating heart, vacant
eyes, nostrils
lacking breath. I want

to stay here, rubbing
your small, frail breast, opening
your mouth, forcing
prayers into your chest—

but then a second kid
bursts the pulsing womb

and stands alone: gray eyes
focused, strong lungs
screaming to be known.

Risks

Say the hip presents—
or some impossible mix
of hoof and head.
Say the pulsing umbilicus
threatens breath.

Perhaps
you're tired;
unqualified to birth
a child. You might
decide the kid
should save itself.

Or, you can
chew your fear
like thrown-up cud,
scrub your hands

(their mid-wife palms
damp, keen, alive),

dive into pain,
free a leg,
pound a failing heart,
clear what's stuck—

and turn
that baby's life around.

Wages

In spring,
you accompany me,
goats the best gardeners—
squatting to water, enriching
earth evenly, clipping
wisps of grass clean.

Amid May bulbs,
you choose the red ones,
pruning all but broad,
limp leaves.

I catch you
with the last stem
in your teeth,
bright garnish for your beard,

and while I shout and stamp
you trot away,
clamp your prize,
nod your head,
and smile.

Milking a Goat Dry

Pink-flecked teats,
stone-dense, peach-
round and almost split.

I work you slowly.
Head pressed against your side,
I clamp, then curl all fingers hard,
your teats between my thumbs and fists,
till both hands coax a bubbling brim,
and leave a bag of limp, wrinkled skin.

Empty!
Can there ever
be more milk?
Blood out of stone?
From silence,
new poems?

But alone,
the miracle:

emptiness
refills.

A Day's Work

You pawed the ground,
I swept the stall,
straw was spread.

You squatted down,
I brought towels,
iodine, thread.

The day was still,
the sun slow and warm;
I fed you quartered
apples, carrot sticks, corn.

And then, thick walls
dissolved, became
a golden jell
that bulged each time
hooves pushed
against the stall.

It streamed like
seaweed hair, hung
like hanks of fleece,
until you screamed, split wide,
I caught a black balloon,
and found
a goat inside—

then heard you grunt,
whine, snort,
chug like trains,
lick, grunt and cry
until your baby
stood; until
your perfect baby dried.

When the Snakes Came

When the snakes came,
wriggling beneath
the dark of our
compost heap,
gliding under vines,
darting at the crunch
of our shoes, sunning
on rocks at the far end
of the garden,

thin, two feet in length,
olive green with lighter
stripes, elusive,
perhaps shy (though I
once felt dry skin
sweep my toes
as I typed in the house,
and saw streaks of chartreuse),

then I knew
we had arrived.
Our ramshackle, weed-rich
land had impressed creatures
who had then chosen us.
Organic, fertile,
our farm was blessed.

Gourmet Eating

I'm dubious
about your diet.
Only grain and hay?

And so I offer
a mixed salad:
a tray of succulent greens;
a spring bouquet.

As your teeth
grind leaves,
I seek young sassafras.
Pungent, three-pronged
and glorious near your beard,
it disappears.

O goat, if we had wings,
imagine trees that we could reach!

Summer

Paint

Visiting,
I pick Van's string beans,
his garden overgrown,
green brush strokes
coarse on the ochre canvas.

A cardinal
lights on his shed.
Streaks of scarlet
stain sienna,
redwood scored
by crimson wings.

His geese
have wandered this way
recently. I see
olive squirts
on the earthen palette.
Soft pellets
line our path.

At peace here,
it is the paint that binds;
waste paint
or rare vermilion—
a squeeze of life
from inside.

Goat De-Horning: What We Do

Rivers of heat rise
from the metal snout,
an iron tongue
with a hunger
for horns.

The vet
ferrets them out,
shaves camouflage,
mows the base
of tiny swords—
weapons
to be taken
in the name of safety.

The red brand
hisses—a thin sound
like spit on kilns—

then hits: bores through
as heat melts bone,
bores again, and leaves

raw craters
ringed with bleeding
coals: a double
crown of thorns.

Grandma

We phoned
the slaughterer, convinced
you had no more to give—
until we saw you help
your daughter kid. Bleating

as when your own does
burst your flesh,
you licked and sponged
until each was clean.

It was so purposefully
domestic: the birth-soaked stall
a small thatched hut;
the floor gleaming
as you brushed;
and heat rising from
your cheerful stove.

As we turned to go,
we caught you teaching
such subtle maternal things—

we phoned
the slaughterer
for your reprieve.

The Elder

The old doe's grown
peevish with time. Pawing

at feed, stomping
at imagined slights,
she even stole her daughter's child.

It sucked dry teat
and almost died. Darting
from dug to shriveled dug
with frantic tongue,
it had to be pulled away
and bottle fed—

while grandma watched
with glazed, bewildered eyes.

The Way It Is

After we sold your bucks
I found you sitting,
just sitting on old straw
in the middle of the yard.

You turned to me,
not knowing it was I
who stole them, made
the phone calls, found
a crate and tied the rope—
so many
rumens to feed,
your milk so rich,
so many reasons why.

I sit beside you,
your small head
suddenly on my knee,
your coarse tongue
scouring my palm for salt—

a thousand crickets mourn,
your cheek feels warm—

I hope that next year
you'll bear does
we'll keep.

The Difference

Twelve ducklings together
are one life: one
pond, one pool
of gold, one lake
of undulating fluff—

like tidal seas
which, though they thin
to rambling streams,
flow back to swell
beneath a mother moon.

One duckling apart
is death
in a pan of mud:

a murky little swim,
a mistimed infant breath,
a lumpy bag, a limp
gray dish-rag.

Naked

Bold, you browse out front,
flecked milk-stone of a goat
mowing weeds near the road.

When I call,
you start for safety,
limp udders bobbing
fitfully as infant fingers.

Near your stall,
you sniff grain
and slow to a sober sway,

your udders then
the dangling sex of men—
men bending over
the sides of a tub in summer,
scouring skin
from last night's bath
with naked hands.

Absolution

Head low,
you lumber out the barn door,
yolk yellow on one clotted haunch,
the other matted:
slimy, drying gray.

Tails toward us,
oblivious ducks peck grain.

You lean meekly
as I scrub your sides,
then kiss your goat-rough cheek.
For I too have crushed other's eggs,
and borne stains
till cleaned.

Elastration

Perhaps
the buck suspects
what he has lost.

His testicles,
now shriveled as leeches,
hang like luck charms
severed, hare-limbs
pinned and swinging
from half-healed holes.
Relics, they dangle
like dead bells.

His mounting is dilatory now,
the memory of old music:
no thrust toward cadence,
no pulse. In time

sperm-stones will fall
and feed the hungry compost;
brace the earth
and make the eggplant grow.

Sacrament

Remnants remain:
stains of blood on back-porch brick;
rope around a low-branched tree;
entrails dragged across the grass;
a table knife we used to free
the pungent pouch from her knee;
acrid musk that was released;
the ax for spine and pelvic bones;
a wild, sweet smell through our clothes;
her powerfully rippling carmine thighs
that gave dark meat we stacked waist high;
the sharp, cracked ribs where she was hit;
the skin we scraped for hours, and soaked
in salt to draw out soul and scent
so that the dark-eyed, gentle doe
could lend her pelt as ornament—

the deer that died in pain
and fear and stillness
when car metal
filled her heart
with splintered bone
till she couldn't feel,
or hear, or see.

Slit Well

The night
we cut the deer for meat,
five pointed teats
mauve buttons
on her tight, bowed belly,
her fawn nowhere in sight,
we didn't expect
milk
mixed with blood
in the gash—

white, bubbling
pockets of flesh,
a sudden tidal-
wet splash,
then a marble
and amethyst
mash.

Flies

Soon,
blue flies
find the dead deer.

With a high-pitched whir
tense as tight wire,
their wild wings
score the air.
Their mica backs glint
like the eyes of the mad.

And when they've sucked
the red meat green,
they pay in pearls:
furrows filled
with future lust
for flesh of the dead—

moist mounds
of slowly moving
maggots.

Duck Releases

When they plopped
into his pristine pool,
Muskovies with their ribald beaks
seemed masked thugs
invading banks for liquid cash.

Then the Pekings waddled near.
Though debonair in plain white coats,
their dive made quite a seismic splash.

My neighbor
raged. Eighty ducks
in suburbia was
insane! He'd phone
the cops.

So I scooped some up
and threw them in my truck.
Past sub-divisions,
strip-malls, bull
dozed barns,
we headed east.

Every fair-sized farm
with a puddle
got some. I'd open
the hatch, haul them out,

send them quacking,
then watch, amazed:
they seemed immediately at home,
not once looking back.

Playing Ball

We perfect out pitch:
cores hurled
against the coop,
crusts chucked
across the fence
and to the pen.

Hens dash in
to fight
for what we've tossed.

Shocked at first,
guests learn the joy
of sharing food with friends,

and so
we sit for hours
in summer, flinging
countless cobs of corn
to hens

who give back
golden yolks
in ivory eggs.

Autumn

The Choice Not Ours

This fall,
leaves are green
as in July,
relaxed as open lips,
sipping lymph from stem

like children,
unaware of want,
drenched in rain
as though such wealth
were birthright,

ignorant of drought—
    the coating of parched tongue,
    the wrinkling of dry skin,

not inured
    as one would be from illness—
    weary, hopeless,
    longing for an end—

and blithely unaware
    that some night soon
    remorseless cold
    will slam cells shut;
    will shrink moist green

to gray, to ragged shards
that dry, then skitter,
blown away.

So the runner,
blood-gorged calves
about to pound the miles
collapses
when a cyst
within his brain
erupts, and life is lost—

the course we cannot choose—
a gradual withering
or a sudden killing frost.

Brief Candle

Made vague by fog,
my house
is a blurred pumpkin.

Its glass smile
sprays the sky
with orange breath.

The night is cold.
Gaunt trees loom
before the distant
glow of home.

I will pass them,
find my door,
and, bathed
in gold awhile,
savor light.

An Aging Breeder's Dream

As I breed rare species,
I conjures caprine trees.

Kids nest
like sweet pears
between leaves.

Entranced among my does,

trunks swell, branches
twine, tendrils dance,
a thousand frisky
progeny prance—

children
I will never have.

Mating

Huge in twilight,
thick coat matted
with semen and pee,
he smells a doe.

Glazed, bulging
as kumquats,
his amber eyes glow.

Rearing, he slams
the fence. His bulk
bends wire, nostrils
flare to inhale night
as her scent
pulls his belly tight
and hardening flesh
begins to pulse.

She in heat,
he can mount
fragrant sheets,
as his blanket
of buck-fur
covers her.

Mated

She comes home drenched
and reeking of buck.
Tossing her head, she stalks
toward feed like a queen.

The other does gather and cling,
nuzzling his smell, grunting
the gossip of hunger

as up she springs,
leaping rocks like sunrise,
beaming.

Purpose

After the hurricane,
the barnyard gleams.
Free of dust,
light sculpts debris.

We chop felled trees,
oaks the wind weeded
with the ease of a snapped finger.
Thick branches break
beneath our blows

and for whole moments,
standing here in sunlight,
our paths are clear
as stacking wood
to warm the coming cold.

The Terror of Locked Doors

Oh, goat, you woke
maddened by fire.

Head thrown back to bray,
your gray tongue bulged.
Food untouched,
you called for hours,
hoarse before brought
to a buck.

But now
you trudge the yard
almost calm.

It is the closing
of the door
of desire.

How can one thrust
shut you, dry dark ropes
that dripped
when you were starved?

Stealthily,
I inch my doors ajar.

What the Stars Are

The buck chased her,
his fullness toward her tail.
When she would not stay,
he reared, hit the sharp
yard rail, and sprayed.

The man in the moon
was like that.

In the dark, he pawed
the earth's soft waist. His fingers
clawed beneath her clouds.

And when she turned away,
he arched his back

and sprayed
the night with stars.

History

Long amber hooves
curl, surround
and lame your feet.

Yet you fight
to keep the very growth
that maims.

As I carve ochre resin
so you contact the ground,

parings fall—
old pain, composted
for the next corporeal round.

Devolution

Experiment.

Toss garden clips and kitchen peel
near sheds out back.

Or broadcast waste for hens to peck
and dogs to gnaw, then defecate.

But alchemy works best
beneath a plastic sheet.
Raise a flap, and you feel heat.
Invade its core—your eyes
are burned by billowing smoke.
Plunge in forks, and pull out
transformation.

So we grow gently
accustomed to our fate—
iron to rust, plant
to soil, flesh
to dust.

The Virtue of Trusting One's Mind

When goats don't want to move,
they don't make sounds.

They fold legs at bald knees,
bend rough necks to earth,
and just sink down.

They never

rant, rail,
protest, declaim,
debate, explain, and then,
head bowed, plod meekly
forward anyway,

as I did
as a child—
and still do now.

Kierkegaard in the Barnyard

At first fade
to graying light,

hens hop to the fence rail
near our spruce and wait.

They glare at blurring space,
shift uncertain feet, peer,
pace, blink ...

then crouch,
flap dubious wings,

and leap—

heave
heavy bodies
upward,

teeter
on supple twigs
that dip,
  rebound,
  careen—

then steady
as they slowly inch
toward sleep.

Productivity

Mornings,
after pregnant sleep,
swollen hens
wait in line
for nesting corners in the barn

and brave
the grinding of goat teeth,
the smack of spongy lips,
goat breath,

because the weight of egg
transcends danger. Poems
drop everywhere:
the need to lay
greater than the fear.

Last Things

For years
the staid red hen—

ancient mother of many eggs
and first on our farm—

would roost in the barn.

Tonight,
she leaps the spruce,
looking prim
against its wild
peeling bark: round
and plump, a ruby
glowing within green.

Without fear
or need of shielding,
she rubs coarse quills
and gulps the naked air of night
to feel its chill.

When stars descend,
they will be sharp; real.

Indecision

This green winter,
this mild December spring;
after ice and sleet, this melting time
can't make up its mind.

Thawed leaves decay
like waning strength
during sweat-drenched fights
in midnight beds.

Dank moss coats trees
like unbrushed teeth
in mouths preoccupied by grief.

Duck droppings freeze
like angry threats
that next day thaw
to spattered pleas,

while young hens search
the earth for sunken feed.

In times like this,
one digs for miles,
and never finds
solid things.

Winter

Transformations

The green world
modulates to white.

Trees streak the primed canvas;
goat-pits dot ice like sheet music;
wisps of straw are gold veins
woven through the snow.

Duck backs are changed
from chalk to mayonnaise,
within bright cold. Cream pelts
have subtle sepia stains.
Dark hens look blue
beside stark snow.

All background space
is clear
as easy breathing.

A touch
transforms
everything we know

Dairyness

Dry fur dusty,
thin flanks hollow
beneath the angle of your hip,
thigh bone knotted
as a stony fist,

all juice seeps sponge-ward,
drips toward the sudden
apotheosis of udder—

like the scholar
who saves passion
for Torah only:
then gives and gives.

The Joys of Milking

Udder fresh,
goat milk tastes clean.

By day two, a leathery coat
of cream, when stirred
and drunk, feels sleek
to the root of our tongues,
a pleasure akin to stroking,
a richness that makes us drink
slowly, swallow
slowly, swallow twice.

Third day, the milk smells
complex and fetid
as Billy-goat stench.

Our immunity grows.
If the goats eat
poison ivy out back,
we never need
Calamine and cortisone.

And when the old
French woman with cancer
believes it is a cure,

we sell her

several quarts a week,
she signing a waiver
swearing the product
(un-pasteurized)
is only for pets.

Magic

A drop of rennet
mixed with milk—
and in an hour
the center gels,
a limpid paste
adrift, like ice
in a pale green sea.

When cut to cubes,
liquid spurts.
Wet oozes
from the huddling clots.
As curds contract,
I pour the pooling
whey to pots,

then wrap the curds
in gauze,
squeeze,
drape on wire
strung over my sink—

and let all slowly

drip,

    until it's dense
        white
            cheese.

Letter

Dear Folks,

Glad you liked the Scobie duck.
He was six months; full grown in size.
Green apples lured him.

He struggled valiantly when caught.
We held his feet and covered his eyes
carrying him, but still he fought.

He did not cry, as some drakes do,
but bashed enormous blue-black wings
until I thought they'd break. At last

he died. We plucked the purest deep-in
down I'd ever seen, beneath
the pearl-gray belly; limp

and light as flakes of snow; as lint
blown from the softest gauze; as fleece
carded clean, and spun. When

I cut into his neck, I felt
a mass. What sudden glad relief
to think him ill, and near a natural

death! I slit his throat,
slipped fingers up, touched the lump,
tugged, looked in, saw shreds

of green—and pulled out several
good sized apple chunks; the ones
that lured him. All other organs

normal. We plucked
and cleaned him. I'm sure
you cooked him well. Our yard

is filled with ducks
we can not keep.

But it is hard to kill.

Grace

We didn't know whom we'd caught,
stalking ducks with fear in our gut
and a hatred of knives.

But we felt willful power
in the way the creature fought;
fiery strength; wild lightning in its eyes.

So we left the head beside our stove,
its onyx gaze framed in carmine folds,

and its hovering soul
saw the skin plucked clean;
watched us spread
spice on the breast, saw
strength pass from flesh
to flesh.

All its fullness
seemed to watch us eat,
hear us praise
wild, pungent meat,
its force incarnate
through the feast.

When we'd sucked
the last bone clean,

its spirit left;
the eye caved in.
Thin blood leaked
from the pearl gray beak.

A light snow fell that night.
We dug a nest through powdery drifts
and buried the head,
so we could rest.

The Passion

The duck dead and gutted,
we walk the vaulted cavity
to the heart; large,
dark, set at the tilt
that till now let it pump.

We dissect the neck
and find blue threads
embedded in the crimson flesh.
A single nick
spills scarlet death.

We unwind entrails,
feeling slippery fat
like topaz dough,
risen and waxed.

As we wrench gall
from liver lobes,
the dripping bile
glows more green
than pine against the whitest snow.

In changing
bird to meat,
we see
    secret things.

The Last Duck

We trapped him—
the dignified male
with the graceful neck—
and held him down
till drowned. His death

was ugly. His heart
wouldn't let his wings
go limp. They hit
the lip of the tub like fists.
There were long slow moments
when we could have let him live.
Then his beak bubbled death,
and we didn't. That day,

a silence stilled the yard.
The ducks didn't fly, drink, eat,
or bob their mobile necks to speak,
but stood, breath-stopped as stone.

In time,
they sought the boulder
he'd used as throne,
exhaled sighs like oboe notes,

and the gargling roll
from the root of their throats
flooded every bite we chewed
of this last duck we killed for food.

Liberation

The last male gone,
the yard falls silent.

There are no more wild meetings,
no gala dances, no stately preening.

There is no violent mating.
Thin necks aren't pierced by beaks.
Fierce eyes aren't numbed by pain.

No quacking audience
encircles the rapes. No more
spent corkscrews drag behind.

There are neither wars between,
nor swaying lines behind
the absent drakes.

All is changed.
The need to nurture gone,
five female ducks
sulk toward spring.

They shuffle leaves,
troll thick mud for bugs,
and often merely sit
and stare. Perhaps

they hear things.
But they never
twitter, groom, greet,
soar on powerful wings—

Sisters! Why
aren't you dancing?
Why don't you sing?

Endurance

Winter nights
they clutch the fir tree,
a whorl of white hens
roosting in the open,
icy nuns
naked before God.

Red combs freeze black,
down feathers swell and spread,
beaks cluck of dreams
the cold winds shred,

but come the day,
they lay their eggs
as usual: summer warm
and whole.

Mucking Out

The one job I hate—

not birthing a kid,
live creature revealed
as fur dries;
not clamping a teat
to squeeze froth;

not bending tree-boughs
as goats browse,
or helping them mate
in the fall. No,

the worst job each week
is mucking the stalls—
heaving the moldering straw
first to the barrow,
then to the mound;
mining deep pockets
of pellet and piss;
starting to sneeze, unable
to breathe for the stench,
for the way my lungs seize
and refuse to unclench—

yet, when all is done
and I sit in the midst

of clean bedding and hay,
my goats like a halo
around what my body's
become, through effort,
asthma, pain—

I feel only thanks
and deep praise.

Digestion

You are passionate
and thorough in your eating.
Loose strands swarm
as you butt the bale,
burrowing
till hay gloves your head
like a hornet's nest.

Then, slowly pulling
choicest clover,
You wait.

Your udders dilate.

So Plato,
sitting at the feet of Socrates,
chewed his tangled lines of thought
and felt the crushed cud
trickle to words:
drop after creamy drop.

Late Milking

After eighteen hours,
her milk retreats
up a solid block of udder.

Her bagpipe teats
feel hollow, dry,
a faint "whoosh"
their only music.

Like waiting too long
to cry. Pain
packs your chest
shut. Voices
speak, faces
blear, but you
remain, remote
and numb,

until steered
to loving fingers
that milk tears.

March Blizzard

White in the wind,
in the whistling music of winter,
feathering trees,
covering corn in the feed bin
lightly, clotting milk
to mounded, icy cream.

Waddling ducks
obscured, their golden beaks
alone make lightning streaks
through white,

and goats
seem reindeer—
crystal-dusted pelts
awaiting sleigh bells;
swollen teats
the only blush
not bleached—

while underneath,
time seeps. Melt

wakes black soil
from sleep,

and stirs
spring.

Change

Rain
breaks the icy
crust of winter.

Drenched feathers cling
to the skin of shivering chickens;
webbed duck-feet slosh
through sludge; leaves stew
in the ooze of earliest spring—

this fearsome, foundering time
before firm ground.

As moths dissolve inside cocoons
till bright, crisp wings emerge,
our visions blear

and are redrawn
through the clear,
kind rain of tears.

Former English teacher and backyard farmer, Marcia Slatkin now plays cello, takes photographs, and writes. *I Kidnap My Mother, Alzheimer Poems* (Finishing Line Press, 2005), depicts a care-giving relationship illuminated by forgiveness and humor. *A Season's Milking* (2003) is the chapbook out of which the present volume grew. Her fiction won two PEN awards and has been published in small magazines. Sixteen of her one-act plays have been produced in small New York venues, and her full length screenplay, *Machete*, survived first cut in the Sundance Film contest, 2004. Children grown, she lives in Shoreham, Long Island, with the mother she "kidnapped" and her partner, Dan. Her website can be found at www.marciaslatkin.com.

Printed in the United States
80559LV00005B/427-474